INVASIVE SPECIES

CANE TOADS

by Alicia Z. Klepeis

pogo

Ideas for Parents and Teachers

Pogo Books let children practice reading informational text while introducing them to nonfiction features such as headings, labels, sidebars, maps, and diagrams, as well as a table of contents, glossary, and index.

Carefully leveled text with a strong photo match offers early fluent readers the support they need to succeed.

Before Reading

- "Walk" through the book and point out the various nonfiction features. Ask the student what purpose each feature serves.
- Look at the glossary together. Read and discuss the words.

Read the Book

- Have the child read the book independently.
- Invite him or her to list questions that arise from reading.

After Reading

- Discuss the child's questions. Talk about how he or she might find answers to those questions.
- Prompt the child to think more. Ask: Cane toads are poisonous. Can you name any other poisonous animals?

Pogo Books are published by Jump!
5357 Penn Avenue South
Minneapolis, MN 55419
www.jumplibrary.com

Library of Congress Cataloging-in-Publication Data

Names: Klepeis, Alicia, 1971- author.
Title: Cane toads / by Alicia Z. Klepeis.
Description: Minneapolis, MN: Jump!, Inc., [2023]
Series: Invasive species | Includes index.
Audience: Ages 7-10
Identifiers: LCCN 2021059789 (print)
LCCN 2021059790 (ebook)
ISBN 9781636907895 (hardcover)
ISBN 9781636907901 (paperback)
ISBN 9781636907918 (ebook)
Subjects: LCSH: Bufo marinus–Juvenile literature.
Introduced amphibians–Juvenile literature.
Classification: LCC QL668.E227 K54 2023 (print)
LCC QL668.E227 (ebook) | DDC 597.8/72–dc23/eng/20211209
LC record available at https://lccn.loc.gov/2021059789
LC ebook record available at https://lccn.loc.gov/2021059790

Editor: Eliza Leahy
Designer: Michelle Sonnek

Photo Credits: Art_man/Shutterstock, cover; Alex Stemmers/Shutterstock, 1, 23; Piotr Naskrecki/Minden Pictures/SuperStock, 3; Minden Pictures/SuperStock, 4; Pete Oxford/Minden Pictures/SuperStock, 5; Jean-Paul Ferrero/Mary Evans Picture Library/SuperStock, 6-7, 14-15; Hans & Judy Beste/Mary Evans Picture Library, 8; Jack Picone/Alamy, 9; Susan Flashman/Shutterstock, 10-11; Zaruba Ondrej/Shutterstock, 12-13; Victor Photo Stock/Shutterstock, 16-17; Julie Thurston/Getty, 17; Joe Raedle/Getty, 18; Auscape International Pty Ltd/Alamy, 19; Ryan M. Bolton/Alamy, 20-21.

Printed in the United States of America at Corporate Graphics in North Mankato, Minnesota.

TABLE OF CONTENTS

CHAPTER 1

HOPPING AND HUNGRY

It's nighttime in northeastern Australia. A toad hops. Its skin is dry. It is covered in warts.

Cane toads can be more than nine inches (23 centimeters) long. Some weigh as much as three pounds (1.4 kilograms). That is about the same weight as a laptop computer!

Cane toads watch their **prey**. They wait for it to get close. Then, they use their sticky tongues to quickly snatch it. This one catches a frog!

DID YOU KNOW?

Cane toads move in short, quick hops. They are not able to jump high.

CHAPTER 2

SPREADING OUT

Cane toads are **native** from southern Texas to South America. In Australia, they are an **invasive species**. So how did they get there? Farmers brought them in on purpose. Cane beetles were eating sugarcane **crops**.

Farmers thought the toads would eat the beetles. But they didn't. Instead, the toads became **pests**, too.

metallic
starling

Cane toads harm their new homes. They put native **predators** at risk. How? They eat the same prey. They hunt frogs, insects, and snakes. They also eat some birds or their **chicks**. Metallic starlings are one.

DID YOU KNOW?

Cane toads mostly eat insects. But they will eat just about anything they can swallow. They will even eat animal poop!

In their native areas, cane toads often live in forests and grasslands. But they can live in deserts and **urban** areas, too. This has helped them spread across Australia.

TAKE A LOOK!

Cane toads are an invasive species in many places around the world. Take a look at some!

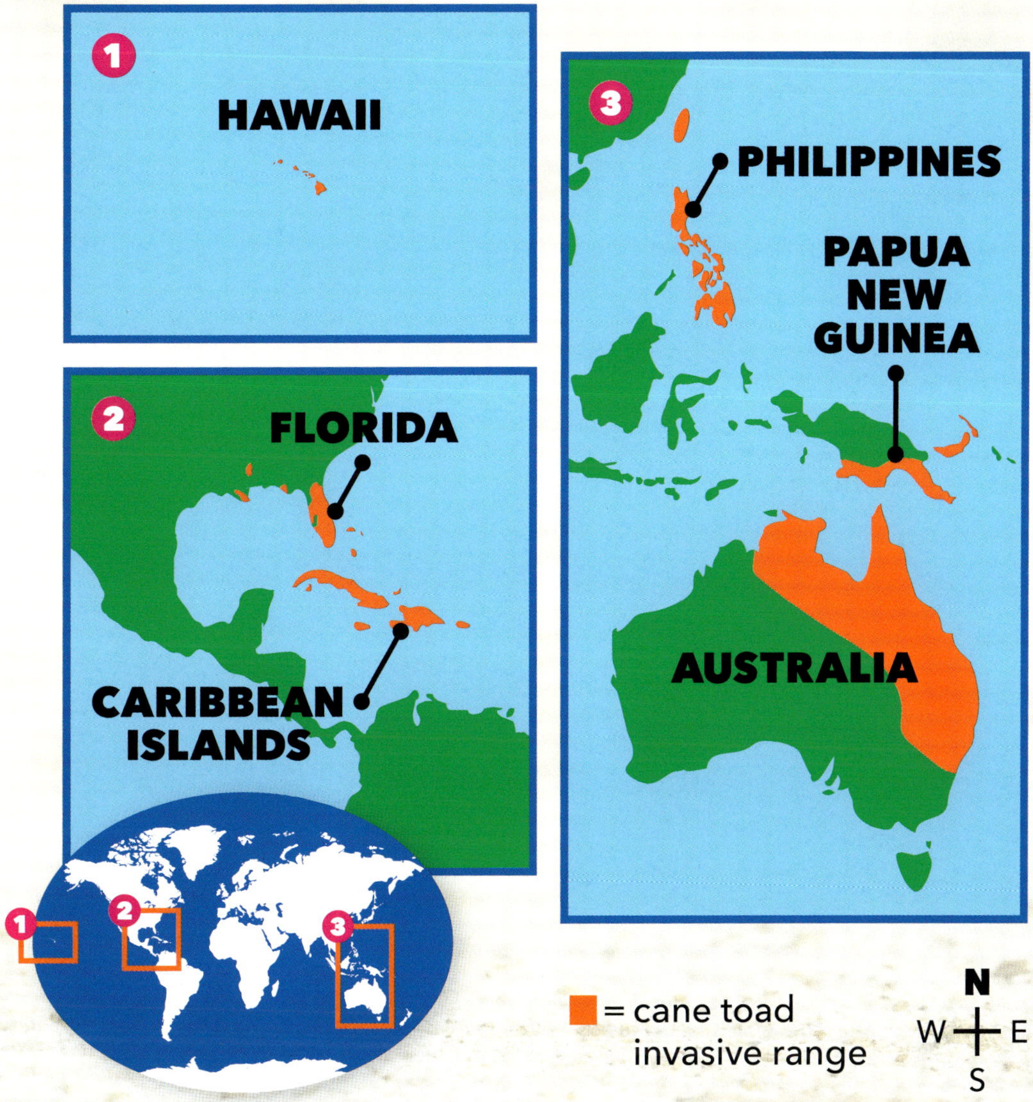

Cane toads have **glands** with **poison** on their backs. It kills animals that try to eat them. This is one reason they have few predators in Australia. Having few predators helps them spread.

DID YOU KNOW?

In Australia, cane toads' bodies are changing. Their legs have gotten longer. They move faster. They spread faster.

poison

eggs

Cane toads produce a lot of young. A female can lay eggs two times each year. She can lay more than 30,000 eggs each time! **Tadpoles** hatch and grow into toads. With so many born at once, the toads can take over a **habitat**. They crowd out native animals. They eat foods native animals depend on.

CHAPTER 3

GO AWAY, CANE TOADS!

Hundreds of millions of cane toads now live in Australia. Scientists work to stop their spread. They trap tadpoles. The tadpoles are then **euthanized**.

The number of northern quolls has dropped since cane toads came to Australia. Many died after trying to eat the toads. Scientists are **breeding** quolls to help increase their numbers.

Cane toads are amazing animals. But they do not belong in Australia.

You can help stop the spread of invasive species. Learn about the frogs and toads that live near you. Grow native plants. The local wildlife will get stronger!

ACTIVITIES & TOOLS

TRY THIS!

INVASIVE SPECIES IN YOUR AREA

Invasive species like cane toads can cause a lot of damage. Learn about invasive species in your area in this activity!

What You Need:

- a computer, books, or magazines
- sheets of paper
- markers, crayons, or colored pencils
- tape or glue
- posterboard or a large sheet of paper

1. **Use a computer, books, or magazines to learn about invasive species in your area. Pick two.**
2. **Learn what these species look like and where they have been found.**
3. **On one sheet of paper, draw a picture of one of the invasive species you chose.**
4. **Repeat Step 3 for the other species.**
5. **Tape or glue your drawings to your posterboard.**
6. **If you are able to use a printer, print out a map of your area. Color in the parts where the invasive species you researched are found.**
7. **What are some similarities between the invasive species you researched and cane toads? What are some differences?**

GLOSSARY

breeding: Keeping animals or plants under controlled conditions so they produce more and better quality offspring.

chicks: Young birds.

crops: Plants that are grown as food.

euthanized: Put to death in a humane manner.

glands: Organs in the body that produce or release natural chemicals.

habitat: A place where an animal or plant is usually found.

invasive species: Any kind of living organism that is not native to a specific area.

native: Growing or living naturally in a particular area of the world.

pests: Insects or animals that destroy or damage crops, food, or livestock.

poison: A substance that can kill or harm a person, animal, or plant if it is swallowed, inhaled, absorbed, or sometimes even touched.

predators: Animals that hunt other animals for food.

prey: Animals that are hunted by other animals for food.

tadpoles: Young toads that live in water and have long tails but no legs.

urban: Having to do with or living in a city.

INDEX

TO LEARN MORE

Finding more information is as easy as 1, 2, 3.

1. Go to www.factsurfer.com
2. Enter "canetoads" into the search box.
3. Choose your book to see a list of websites.

FACT SURFER